GOLF LEGENDS

John Daly

Golf Stars of Today

Jack Nicklaus

Greg Norman

Arnold Palmer

Tiger Woods

CHELSEA HOUSE PUBLISHERS

GOLF LEGENDS

JOHN DALY

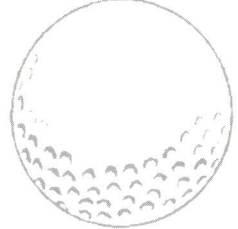

Martin J. Mooney

CHELSEA HOUSE PUBLISHERS
Philadelphia

Produced by Daniel Bial and Associates
New York, New York

Picture research by Alan Gottlieb
Cover illustration by Bill Vann

Copyright © 1999 by Chelsea House Publishers, a division of Main Line Book Co. All rights reserved. Printed and bound in the United States of America.

First Printing

1 3 5 7 9 8 6 4 2

Library of Congress Cataloging-in-Publication Data

Mooney, Martin J.
    John Daly / by Martin Mooney
       p. cm. — (Golf legends)
    Includes bibliographical references and index.
    Summary: A biography of the golfer whose tactics and behavior have shocked his opponents, but who proved his ability by winning the British Open in 1995.
      ISBN 0-7910-4581-1 (hc)
    1. Daly, John, 1966–   —Juvenile literature. 2. Golfers—United States—Biography—Juvenile literature. [1. Daly, John, 1966–   .
2. Golfers.] I. Title. II. Series.
GV964.D26M66   1998
796.352'092—dc21
[B]   97-46464
                                                                                 CIP
                                                                                  AC

CONTENTS

CHAPTER 1
THE OLD COURSE   7

CHAPTER 2
A TALENTED BOY   15

CHAPTER 3
HOME TO ARKANSAS   21

CHAPTER 4
GOING PRO   29

CHAPTER 5
CROOKED STICK   37

CHAPTER 6
HAZARDS   45

CHAPTER 7
THE LONG ROAD BACK   55

STATISTICS   61
CHRONOLOGY   62
FURTHER READING   63
INDEX   64

1
THE OLD COURSE

Dancing with his wife, listening to the music of Wilson Pickett, and eating a half-dozen chocolate croissants, John Daly began his day. The day was Sunday, July 23, 1995, and Daly stood at the threshold of what would be the most important round of golf in his career, the fourth round of the British Open at the birthplace of golf, The Royal and Ancient Golf Club at St. Andrews, Scotland. How did he prepare? By eating doughnuts and cavorting around his hotel room to "Land of a Thousand Dances." This is probably not the way the legends of the game, men such as Bobby Jones, Ben Hogan, Arnold Palmer, or Jack Nicklaus, would have begun their day. But their time had passed, and this day would belong to the 29-year old from Dardanelle, Arkansas.

The road to St. Andrews was a rocky one for

John Daly had one of his greatest successes at the 1995 British Open. He won the tournament despite missing a birdie putt on this hole.

John Daly. When he burst upon the professional golf scene with a victory at the PGA (Professional Golfers Association) Championship in 1991, he was heralded as the next in a long line of great American golfers. However, at 25, he was not yet ready to handle all of the fame and media attention that followed his victory at the PGA Championship. Since that victory, he had only won two other tournaments and had a slew of personal and professional difficulties to overcome. Many felt that he might never fulfill the immense potential he had shown in the 1991 PGA Championship.

On this day, Daly was feeling good about his game again. On Thursday, he had shot an eye-opening 67 and followed it with a fine 71 on Friday, which put him on top of the leader board tied for first place with fellow American Brad Faxon and Japan's Katsuyoshi Tomori, all at six strokes under par.

Few had expected Daly to star here. Daly's strength is his driving—he's regularly the longest driver on the PGA tour. But Scottish courses don't reward long drivers the way American courses do. In Scotland, the courses aren't perfectly manicured; careless golfers will have their ball bouncing in crazy directions off the hillocks and irregularities in the terrain. Experts felt that Daly, with his let-'er-rip style, couldn't control the ball well enough to compete against more careful players—and some experts doubted that Daly could even control himself well enough nowadays.

When the third round began on Saturday, a stiff breeze—what the Scots would call a "freshening wind"— blew out of the north to greet the competitors who had made the cut. At the end of the second round, only a certain number of golfers are permitted to play in the final two rounds. Those with scores within a certain range are the ones who "make the cut." Daly performed well, shooting a one-over-par 73, a good score in these conditions, but not good enough to hold onto the lead. The hero on Saturday was Michael Campbell, a 26-year-old from New Zealand, who shot a 65, seven strokes under par. His score was the lowest of the tournament and three strokes better than anyone else that day. The descendant of a Scotsman, Campbell drew many cheers from the crowd; St. Andrews has not seen a Scot win the tournament in the 20th century, so anyone with a name that was even remotely Scottish drew thunderous applause on the Old Course.

As good as Campbell was on Saturday, he was equally bad on Sunday. Finding trouble in St. Andrews' notorious bunkers and three-putting a number of times, by the time he finished the front nine, Campbell had dropped three strokes and the lead. The man who had captured the imagination of the gallery at the Royal and Ancient Golf Club shot a five-over-par 76 and finished at minus 6 for the tournament, one stroke behind the fourth-round leaders.

As Campbell relinquished the lead, John Daly picked up the slack. By the 10th hole, Daly had slugged his way back to a two-stroke lead. He was poised to capture his second major championship. The only things that stood between him and the silver claret jug—the trophy of this tournament—were nine rugged holes of golf and an Italian named Constantino Rocca.

By the 13th hole, Daly had built up a three-stroke lead, but veterans of the tournament knew

Daly walks off the 18th hole with Constantino Rocca after defeating Rocca in a playoff.

that this was a golf course that could bring even the most celebrated golfers in the world to their knees. On Thursday, Jack Nicklaus had quintuple bogeyed—which means he shot five strokes over par—on the 14th, a par five with an unforgiving trap called the Hell Bunker; a 10 for the Golden Bear, arguably golf's greatest player ever, was unheard of. On Friday, Bill Glasson, who shared the lead when he teed up on the 17th, saw his lead go up in flames as he took an eight; he plunged from 1st to 20th place in one hole. With obstacles like these yet to come, the toughest going was clearly ahead for Daly.

There were many who were waiting for Daly's game to crumble. It was no secret that Daly, with his "good old boy" mannerisms, outlandish personality, and lack of proper golf etiquette—he became famous for eating gargantuan amounts of cookies and doughnuts while playing his rounds—had his detractors. Golf's older, more conservative establishment was reluctant to accept this barbarian into their exclusive club. After Daly bogeyed the 16th, his lead was two strokes going into the toughest hole on the Old Course, the par-four 17th.

When he approached the tee with his driver in his hand, many students of the game probably cringed. With a two-shot lead on the most difficult hole, the conventional wisdom is to play the hole safely, hit a one- or two-iron off the tee, and be happy with par. The idea is to sit on your lead, and make the other guy, in this case Constantino Rocca, beat you by having to make two birdies. (A "birdie" is golfers' language for shooting one stroke under par for a hole; an "eagle" is two strokes under; a "bogey" is one stroke over.) However, "conventional" and "safe" are not words in John Daly's golfing dictionary. This is the man who coined the phrase "grip it and rip it," meaning John Daly just tees up his ball, gets a good grip on his club, and hits it ("rips it") as hard as he can.

Feeling the pressure of the moment, Daly drove into the rough on the 17th. After scrambling out of trouble there, he found himself in the treacherous Road Bunker but chipped onto the green and two-putted for bogey. Rocca had his own problems on 17, but with a miraculous putt from the road, he remained cool and collected, parred the hole, and moved to within one stroke of the lead. As long as Daly continued to make bogeys, Rocca would have a chance on the 18th hole.

After making a safe par on the 18th, all Daly could do was watch as Rocca approached the tee. Up to this point in his career, Rocca was most remembered for blowing a sure victory against the United States' Davis Love III in the 1993 Ryder Cup. (The Ryder Cup is a match-play tournament in which a U.S. team competes against a team of European professionals.) Rocca's loss was seen as the one that turned the tide for the American team, who eventually went on to win the Cup.

Rocca teed up the ball and drove it up the left side of the fairway, almost reaching the green. Needing a birdie to force a playoff with Daly, Rocca attempted a simple chip shot to the green. He hoped to put the ball as close as possible to the hole, which would give him the chance to putt for birdie. However, Rocca flubbed his chip shot, mis-hitting the ball terribly. It flew for only a few feet and then rolled for only about 25 more. The shot left Rocca in the Valley of Sin, a deep and tricky depression in the green. Now, instead of a straight, makable 10-footer, he would have to sink a 65-foot, almost impossible, putt to earn a playoff with Daly.

Not far from the green, Daly, his wife, Paulette, and his caddie, Greg Rita, watched in disbelief. After all of the trials and tribulations; after being suspended by the PGA twice; and after numerous personal problems, all that stood between Daly and the British Open Championship was 65 feet of Scottish sod. Hugging and kissing after Rocca's last shot, Daly and Paulette allowed themselves to relax, knowing that making such a putt was nearly impossible.

They celebrated too soon. Rocca stunned everyone by draining the 65-footer right into the center of the hole and forced a four-hole playoff.

Daly's reaction was one of disbelief. After feeling as if the tournament was his, Daly could not believe he would be fighting for the Championship in a four-hole playoff round, a round that would put the two golfers against each other on holes 1, 2, the dreaded 17, and 18.

Would Daly now finally play it safe? Would he keep the famous "Killer Whale" driver in his bag as many of his peers would have done? Would the man they call "Wild Thing" finally be tamed? No. Believing that he must remain true to his skills and use the tactics that had brought him to the playoff in the first place, John Daly attacked the Old Course. Rather than play safely and hope that Rocca would make mistakes, John Daly followed his own voice. That voice was telling him what it had told him his whole life: "Grip it and rip it."

In the playoff, Daly hit the ball like a man possessed. He parred the first hole, just missing a birdie putt; Rocca bogeyed it. On the second hole, Daly rolled in a 35-foot putt for birdie, which seemed to take much of the starch out of Rocca, who made his par. Down two strokes going into the nightmarish 17 was most likely too much for Rocca; when he saw Daly pull the driver out of his bag and rip a monstrous 345-yard drive down the middle of the fairway, he must have had an idea the tournament was over. When Rocca landed his drive in the Road Bunker on 17, took three strokes to get out, and three-putted for a seven, he removed all doubt.

Going into the final hole of the playoff with a five-stroke lead, John Daly could almost relax. However, this was a treacherous course, and anything could happen. It was not until he sank his par putt that Daly could finally celebrate his victory. On the most famous golf course in the world, Daly had established himself as a champion who could win anywhere, any time.

Daly kisses the British Open trophy. His victory meant he would never be considered a one-shot golfer.

2
A TALENTED BOY

When John Daly was three years old, his father Jim gave him a shortened club and set him up to hit his first golf ball. Just out of diapers, the young Daly stepped up and gave the ball a mighty whack. So powerful was the swing, in fact, that the ball flew 30 yards and broke the family room window in the Daly house.

At the time, John's family lived in Sacramento, California, where Jim Daly was a nuclear engineer. His business would require him to move to a number of different places during John's childhood. When John was five, his family moved to Dardanelle, Arkansas; when he was 10, they relocated to Virginia; and by the time he was ready to enter ninth grade, the family moved to Zachary, Louisiana.

Because the family moved around so much, John had developed a shy and reserved per-

John Daly was always big for his age. In high school, he was a fine football kicker, although his nickname was the Pillsbury Dough Boy.

sonality. Always being the new kid on the block forced John to make his own fun much of the time. John quickly found out that he not only enjoyed golf, but he was also good at it.

By the time John was nine, he was beating his father on a regular basis. At the age of 13, while living in Virginia, he won his first club championship—not a junior championship, but a club tournament against men much older and more experienced in golf than he.

The family remained in Zachary, Louisiana, for a year and a half, but in the middle of John's sophomore year in high school, the Dalys moved to Jefferson City, Missouri.

Compared to where the Dalys lived in Arkansas, Virginia, and Louisiana, Jefferson City was a sprawling urban center. Jefferson City High School, where John was enrolled for only a few days, boasted over 2,000 students. John seemed overwhelmed by the size and the atmosphere of the large high school. After a few days his mother arranged for him to transfer to the smaller Helias High School, a Catholic school with a growing reputation as an athletic and academic powerhouse.

As it would happen many times afterward, John's reputation preceded him at Helias. Word had gotten out that this young man could really hit the ball. So when the golf coach at Helias, Ray Hengtes, finally got a chance to take a look at how the kid could play, the anticipation was great. The first time he teed up the ball for his first practice round, with his new coach and new teammates watching him intently, John got a case of nerves. He did not hit the ball with the customary Daly explosiveness; as a matter of fact he topped the ball, crunching it directly into

A Talented Boy

Daly led his high school golf team to a state championship in 1983. Members of the team included (from left): Scott Cassmeyer, Chris Hentges, coach Ray Hentges, Daly, and Brad Struttman.

the grass, for a grand total of about 80 yards. Luckily, Daly recovered his poise and ended up shooting one-under-par for the round.

The season that followed was an extremely strong one for John and for the team. Helias finished with a record of 66-7, and John took third place in the State Championship.

The following year was an even stronger one for John in a number of ways. Off the course, he had a tight circle of friends, including Chris Hengtes, the son of the golf coach. Chris was a talented golfer, but football and wrestling were his main sports. In fact, he owned many of the school's rushing records in football. Because of his athletic success and his clean-cut image,

In high school, Daly liked going out to an open field to practice his driving form.

Chris was a popular kid at Helias. Being friends with someone so popular was a new experience for John, who had never had many friends. He and Chris spent a lot of time together, both on and off the course.

With good friends around him and another successful season in the spring of 1983—Helias' record was 66-9, and they won the state championship—John was flying high. He and Chris Hengtes were such good friends that Chris agreed to caddy for John at the Missouri State Amateur Golf Championship in 1983. This was not a high school tournament; it was open to any amateur in the state, and John would be competing against men far older and more experienced than himself. But as he had proved as a 13-year-old in Virginia, he was equal to the task. Scorching the rest of the field, John shot eight under par for the tournament, winning the Missouri amateur championship at the young age of 17.

Such early success did not make John cocky or proud off the course. In fact, when he was not playing golf, John was self-conscious and unsure of himself. He had gained a lot of weight since coming to Jefferson City. It did not help matters that Coach Hengtes had a standing bet with his team that he would buy dinner for any player who beat his score on the days the team had matches. (Many times golf coaches will play a round behind their teams during a match.) John was often a recipient of an extra burger and fries when the team stopped to eat.

In spite of his appetite, John was still a fairly

good athlete, and because of John's size and his ability to kick the football, Chris convinced John to try out for the football team in his senior year. With Chris Hengtes leading the way at running back, the Crusaders went a perfect 10-0. John was as much a factor in that season as a kicker could be; he even kicked 10 extra points in one game.

In the last game of the season, John had to do something he had not wanted to do all year. He was reluctant to play football because of what an injury might do to his golf game. As a kicker he never really had to worry about contact, and on kickoffs he really tried to stay out of the fray. Only with time running out in the final game of the year, John could not avoid contact any longer. An opposing running back was going in for a score, which would have seriously jeopardized Helias's perfect record. However, John was able to get a good angle on the running back and make a game-saving tackle.

John began to hang out with a different group of friends, one that didn't include his friend Chris. He and his brother Jim were often left on their own when their parents were out of town on business. With John's insecurity and the lack of supervision, and with the influence of Chris reduced, it was only a matter of time before he started getting into trouble. Trouble came in the form of beer, which he experimented with in high school. This was the beginning of a long struggle with alcohol, a struggle that would take a serious toll on Daly's personal and professional life.

3
HOME TO ARKANSAS

It had always been John Daly's dream to play golf at the University of Arkansas. Arkansas had been the Daly ancestral home—his grandfather had lived in the house in Dardanelle where the Dalys moved when John was five—and John had lived there long enough to consider it home. The five years he spent there were the longest stretch of time he and his family stayed in any one place.

John had been promised an athletic scholarship to play golf at the University of Arkansas, but only if he was a state resident. If he did not leave Jefferson City in the middle of football season, he would not be able to claim state residency.

In March 1984, John and his brother Jamie set up house in Arkansas. John enrolled at Dardanelle High, while his brother looked after him, finding work here and there in construction. Jamie had graduated from Helias the year before.

College coach Steve Loy gives John Daly some pointers.

The two young men lived together for those months by themselves. John's parents did not move back to Arkansas with the boys; Jim's job took him back on the road, this time to New Hampshire.

At Dardanelle, John concentrated more on his game than he did on doing well in school. While he did graduate, he did not attend the graduation ceremony. Instead, he played in a golf tournament.

His summer was spent playing golf, eating, and enjoying the life of a young man who has everything planned out. He would tell his friend Rick Ross, the pro at the Bay Ridge Boat and Golf Club, the local golf club where John spent much of his time that summer, that he would someday be playing in the pros. This was nothing new for John; he had made this prediction to anyone who would listen back in Jefferson City. But Rick was different. He took John's pronouncement seriously, and he also knew first hand how difficult it was to make it as a pro. For every Jack Nicklaus or Arnold Palmer on the tour, there are hundreds of very good golfers making a living by giving lessons at golf courses all over America.

Rick Ross became a mentor of sorts for John. He certainly was the first person who was able to successfully teach John to control his massive swing. He was the person who tried to make John see that having control of his life would translate into having control over his game. Rick remains a true friend and guide for John to this day.

Fresh off the heels of winning the Arkansas Amateur State Championship—his second in two states in two years—John set out for

Fayetteville, the home of the University of Arkansas. The University, which built a reputation as a football powerhouse in the 1960s and 1970s, was able to ride that fame to success in its other sports, specifically track, basketball, and with the hiring of Steve Loy, success in golf in the early 1980s.

Steve Loy was the man who recruited John to come to the University, and he was the man who looked at John with a little displeasure when he arrived on campus quite overweight. After a summer of eating and drinking and playing golf, John came to school weighing a hefty 235 pounds.

Steve Loy's approach to the game of golf was more like a football coach's. He had a meticulous and detailed practice regimen, which his players had to follow to the letter. For the first time in his life, someone was forcing John to work on his short game and his putting. This was far from the practice tee back at Jefferson City, where John would take bets on how far he could hit the ball. John was now playing for a man who told his players which clubs to play on individual holes in tournaments. Although every coach has the right to coach how he sees fit, this approach did not sit too well with John, who was to become one of the most untraditional players in a very traditional sport.

Coach Loy also put John on a strict diet, made him weigh in on a regular basis, and made him work out every day—and not just with his driver. Because both golf and being at the University were so important to him, John did what he had to do. After three months, his weight came down to about 175 pounds. He told the *Arkansas Gazette*, "I was fat, immature, and sensitive. I needed the discipline it takes in losing the weight and maintaining it."

Even though he kept the weight off in his freshman year, John did not play very much. Because of John's temper and immaturity, Steve Loy did not insert him into the lineup on a regular basis. Their relationship came to a head during the qualifying round of the Southwest Conference Tournament. John threw a sand wedge after flubbing a bunker shot. Loy picked up the club, and trying to teach his temperamental student a lesson, struck John in the leg with it.

Although John and Steve would never have the best of relationships, the following year was much better for John. He became more in tune with his game and what was expected of him at this level. His run-ins with the coach were fewer, and he found himself on the leader board of many more tournaments in his sophomore year. He culminated that year by finishing fourth at the Southwest Conference Tournament and earning the 14th spot at the NCAAs. In the third round of that tournament John distinguished himself by setting a new course record of 65 at the Bermuda Run course in Raleigh, North Carolina.

After his impressive performance at the NCAA Tournament and after finishing very well in local qualifying rounds, in 1986 John earned the right to play in the U.S. Open Championship at Shinnecock Hills on Long Island. At the age of 20, John would be playing as an amateur in one of the most prestigious tournaments in the world, at one of the oldest and most beautiful golf courses in the United States. Shinnecock Hills, nestled between the Atlantic Ocean to the south and the Hampton bays to the north, was known for

HOME TO ARKANSAS

Bill Woodley, Daly's second coach at the University of Arkansas, was bothered by Daly's drinking and wanted him to get help.

its long fairways, its unforgiving rough, and its winds, which ripped across the course with little regard for the people who were foolish enough to try and hit a little white ball on it.

Shinnecock was also the place where John first met his idol, Jack Nicklaus—sort of. Before the start of the first round, John was on the practice tee getting ready to hit. He looked up, and when he did, the Golden Bear said "hi" to him. For all his insecurities off the course, John was always confident on it; yet when Nicklaus, the man he had always tried to emulate, the man who at age 46 had just won the Masters for the sixth time, the man who had spawned the greatest golf revival the game had ever known, said "hi" to him, John was too starstruck to say anything. "When he spoke to me, I was so shook, so in awe, I couldn't say a word back."

John did not seem to get over the awe of being in his first major tournament that day. He knew it was probably going to be a long day when he

Daly practices his putting in preparation for a big opportunity. In 1986, Daly qualified to play in the U.S. Open.

had to tee off at 3:00 in the afternoon while an afternoon storm was descending on the Hamptons. His "luck" on the fourth hole set the tone for the rest of the round. Because it was so late in the day and the spotters had gone in for the afternoon, John lost two balls in the deep rough and he took the "snowman," golfer slang for an 8. By the end of the round, he had shot an 18-over-par 88. The following day he carded a respectable 76. Although he did not make the cut in his first major, he did gain some valuable experience. He told the *Arkansas Gazette* that evening, "I'm glad I stayed with it and never gave up. I just want the state to know that I tried up here and never gave up."

When John returned to Arkansas for his junior year, he had a new coach. Bill Woodley, the former head coach for the Horned Frogs of Texas Christian University, replaced Steve Loy, who moved on to coach at Arizona State. Woodley, who stressed the personal nature of the game of golf, was very different from Loy. While Loy felt that a coach could control the game for his players, Bill Woodley felt that the game was one of individual choice and intuition.

This style appealed to the freewheeling John Daly at first, but he would have his differences with Coach Woodley. Woodley was bothered by Daly's drinking, which sometimes got out of hand.

Demonstrating a true concern for John's health and well-being, Woodley suggested that John try to get some help for his alcohol dependence. John bristled at this intrusion in his life, and soon after decided to leave the University.

After being the number one golfer and an All-American in his sophomore and junior years, John announced in late July 1987 that he would be turning pro.

4
Going Pro

When John Daly announced that he was leaving the University of Arkansas and trying his game in the professional ranks, there was more than a little agitation in Fayetteville. Coach Bill Woodley, the man who tried to help John gain control of his game and his personal life felt betrayed—or at least confused.

Daly told the local media that he was leaving because he felt slighted that he was the number one player but wasn't receiving a full scholarship—although he didn't tell that to his coach. John did receive a full scholarship but had to pay for books. Woodley told the *Arkansas Democrat*, "John was very vague about his reasons for turning pro when he called to talk to me on Wednesday. He didn't express any dissatisfaction to me."

John gave three reasons for turning pro. First, he felt so focused on becoming a professional

---

In 1986, Daly was voted Arkansas Golfer of the Year.

that he was "afraid I wouldn't go to class very much for my senior year. And I think that would jeopardize my grades and keep me from ever coming back to get my degree." He also felt he was playing about as well at this point as he could. The third reason was, "My parents are really behind me on this. They believe I can make it and so do I."

Whatever the reasons he gave, being a professional golfer was what he had wanted to do his whole life, and now was the time to pursue that dream.

Filled with the confidence and enthusiasm of one who is pursuing a dream but who has not yet seen the real pitfalls, John became a professional during the summer of 1987. At the age of 21 he was finally making a living out of being a golfer.

If his first year as a professional had been as successful as his first few weeks, John would have made the PGA Tour in no time. In his first tournament as a pro, John won the Missouri Open in Columbus and did well enough in two other tournaments, in Arkansas and Oklahoma, to earn $17,000. The young long-driver from Arkansas must have thought that this thing could not be easier. Then he went to the 1987 PGA Qualifying Tournament.

Being a professional golfer at the highest level, the PGA, is not unlike being any other kind of professional athlete. To earn a spot on the Tour, one must be among the "best of the best." Just like a pro football camp or spring training in baseball, golf has its own way to sift out the best players: the qualifying tournament. Held every fall, the qualifying tournament is a series of rounds in which the number of golfers is reduced every week; just like in football or baseball, these are cuts. Only the best get to participate in the finals, a grueling six-round tournament. When John Daly entered his first PGA Qualifying Tournament, he would be facing all the other "wannabes" from across America. Every guy who had won a club championship or state tournament, was the number one player on his college team, or had picked up a few dollars in low-level professional play was there looking to do one thing: earn his PGA touring card. This would allow him to play in just about any PGA-sanctioned event he wanted to.

John started out well in the qualifying process. He made it through the first round easily, then did well enough in the second to move on to the third and final phase, which was held in Florida. However, John did not make the final cut. His year would be filled with lesser tournaments in cities that had been bypassed by the major tours, and he would be playing in front of relatively few people. However, it was golf, and it was a living, so John trudged on. At the next year's qualifying tournament, he was again eliminated in the final round.

Faced with the reality of playing another year of nickel-and-dime tournaments and maybe lucking into a PGA event with a special sponsor exemption, John decided to go overseas to play golf. Through contacts with former teammates at Arkansas, John was able to earn a spot on the South African tour. It was an opportunity for him to earn more money, gain more experience, and play in front of more fans than he would if he stayed in the United States for another year. The tour began in December and ran through February, the summertime in the South-

In 1991, Daly became engaged to Bettye Fulford. Fulford was six years older than Daly and tried to help him through his personal problems.

ern Hemisphere. By the end of the season, John had earned over $20,000.

Daly returned to the States a few dollars richer and with a new sense of himself as a professional. His success on the tour carried over into his career back in America, and the following summer he was able to qualify for the U.S. Open for the second time.

Held at the Oak Hill Country Club in Rochester, New York, the Open offered top competition, but Daly was up to the challenge. His scores of 74 and 67 were good enough for him to make the cut in only his second appearance at a major championship. It was his biggest thrill so far as a pro. Well, maybe his second biggest.

John finished the tournament poorly, shooting 80 and 79 over the weekend, combining for a 20-over-par for the tournament, but he once again ran into his boyhood idol, Jack Nicklaus. This time, Jack just watched John's swing on the practice range and winked at him. John also netted a $4,000 paycheck.

Using a network of friends and contacts, John was able to enter other PGA events, even though he did not have his card yet, because a certain number of spots needed to be filled, usually with local pros. John played in a number of PGA tournaments this way and began to earn the friendship of tour veterans.

Although his career was not where he wanted it to be, between stops on the South African Tour, any PGA Tour exemptions he could get, and whatever long-drive contests he could win, he was making a living. The problem he was having these days came not on the course, but in his personal life. After leaving Arkansas, he met a girl named Dale Crofton and immediately fell in love. The two were married not long afterward. However, being the wife of a touring pro was not the life Dale wanted, and she and John divorced in 1989.

After the divorce, Daly fell into a funk and began drinking heavily. He sought help and started to drink less, but alcohol would be a problem that would reappear.

Ready to compete again in early 1990, John went back to South Africa. The courses there were big and beautifully long—tailor-made for Daly's big drive off the tee and his overall long game.

Shooting a course record of 62 in the third round of a tournament at Johannesburg's Rand Park, John went on to win his first tournament on what was called the Sunshine Tour, earning

$16,000 for the weekend. Two weeks later he won in Swaziland, and in March he came in third in two tournaments. His success led him to be invited to the South African Skins game, a four-man match in which on each hole prize money (the "skin") is awarded to the player with the lowest score. If there is a tie, the money is carried over to the next hole. John won an additional $35,000 at this event.

With his new success, John decided to try to qualify for a new tour that would be sort of a "farm system" for the PGA. It was called the Ben Hogan Tour, a regular tour meant for professionals who were not quite ready for the PGA Tour, and who did not want to have to travel to places like South Africa or Asia to make a living and gain experience. Things were looking up when John won the qualifying tournament.

The great thing about the Hogan tour is that the PGA guarantees that the top five money winners will automatically make the big leagues. In addition, the next 45 players on the money list were given special consideration at the PGA Qualifying Tournament, such as being allowed to skip the preliminary tournaments and go right to the final. Knowing that this was his best chance to finally get his PGA card, John set out to conquer the Hogan Tour.

Even though John had a rough time of it at the beginning of the tour—like the time he shot a 91 at a tour stop in Maine, which submerged John into such a deep depression that he took a couple of weeks off to clear his mind—by the end of the summer he was playing like a champion again. Living out of his car in the summer of 1990, he won the Utah Open and finished second in the Texarkana and Arkansas Opens in

August. Even though he was very successful on the tour, he did not finish in the top five money winners; he would have to go back to the Qualifying Tournament. However, he did make enough money to skip right into the final round, in which he finished 12th. He was now eligible to play in just about every PGA-sanctioned event in 1991.

John credited his improved playing to his new love, Bettye Fulford, whom he had met at a tour event in Georgia. Although she was a little bit older than John—30 years to his 24—the two felt a kinship. In addition, Bettye watched out for John and tried to keep him out of trouble, with varying amounts of success. Nevertheless, Bettye would be by his side as he entered this extremely crucial time in his career.

This was a crucial time for John because he was an aggressive player and had not learned how to lose well. The qualifying tournament would be a big step in his career, but it could offer nothing more than the hope for better paydays ahead. After all, the tournament was filled with players who had earned a one-year exemption, but because they did not finish among the top 125 money winners for the year they had to do the whole thing all over again.

"The key for John is to keep making the cuts and beating on the door and eventually the door is going to open," said friend Fuzzy Zoeller. "But for now he needs to just not rush it." This was good, sound advice from a veteran pro to a young man tackling golf or any other profession. The message was clear: Stay focused, stay with your game, and do not be too upset if success does not follow right away. Yet the question remained: Would John Daly follow Zoeller's advice?

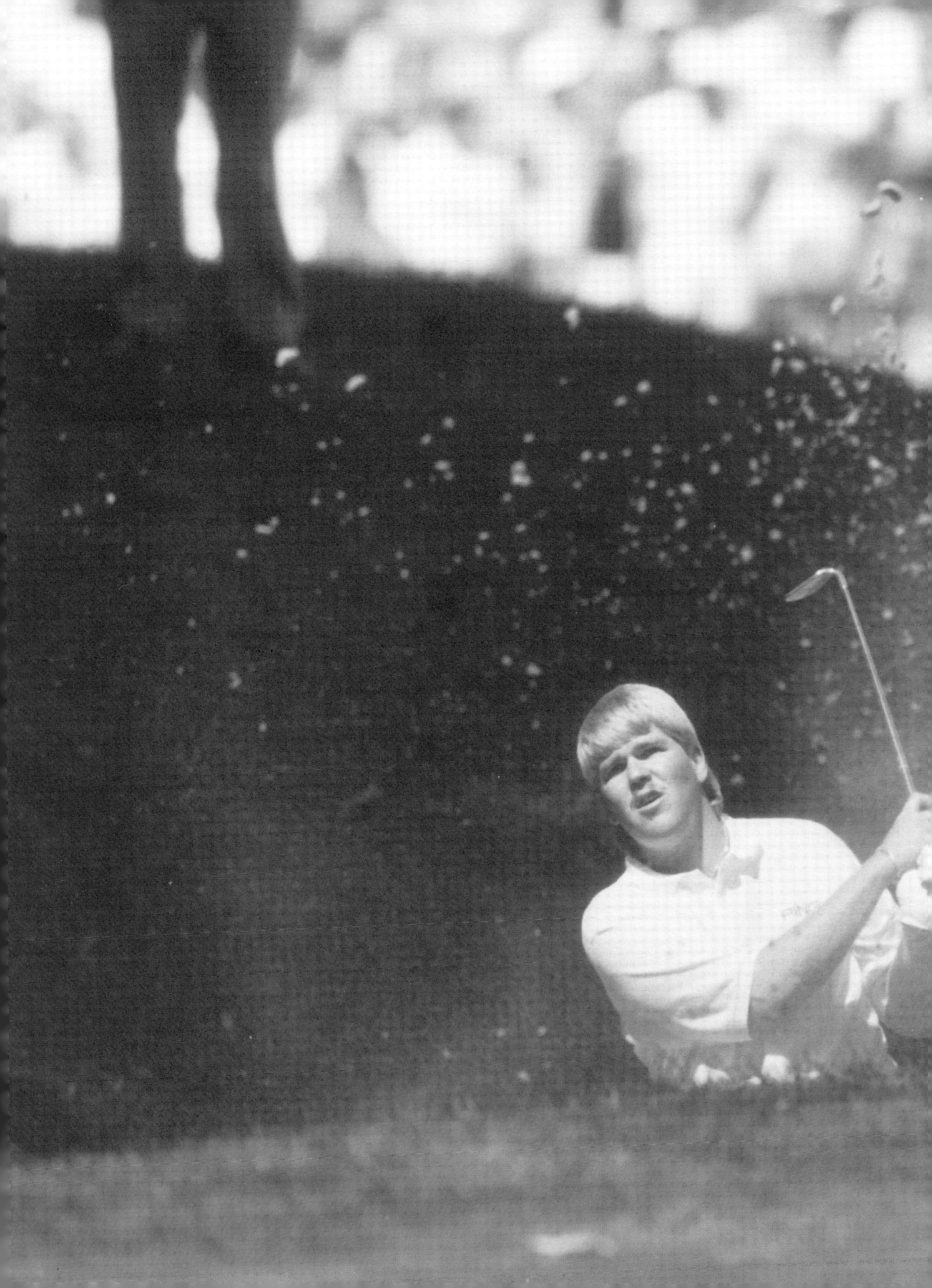

5
CROOKED STICK

In 1991, the PGA Championship, which is the last of the four major tournaments, was held at the Crooked Stick Golf Course in Carmel, Indiana, just outside Indianapolis. The PGA Championship is sort of like Labor Day in the golf world; held in mid-August, it signals that the end of the season is at hand. It is the last big tournament of the season, and because of that, it attracts a lot of attention.

When August came around, John had put some good tournaments together and was 72nd on the money list, practically ensuring himself another year's exemption on the PGA Tour. He was feeling so good about his fortunes that he went out the week before the PGA and bought Bettye a red BMW. Things were going well for Daly, but the BMW was probably pushing it; however, he told friends that he liked "living on the edge."

Daly blasts out of the bunker at the 1991 PGA Championship. He was glad simply to have been invited to participate in the tournament.

When the PGA Championship field was announced, Daly was not in it. He was chosen as the ninth alternate—way down at the bottom of the list. It was not uncommon for tour rookies to get bumped from the majors, especially the PGA Championship, which reserved a number of spots for full-time teaching professionals. When the week began, he decided he was too far down on the alternates list to even make the trip from Memphis, where he and Bettye had built a house, to the tournament in Indianapolis.

However, much to Daly's delight, his name rose on the list of alternates as players began to drop from the tournament. When Nick Price's wife went into labor on the day before the Championship began, John was given his chance. He and Bettye drove the red BMW all night to reach Crooked Stick by Thursday morning. John did not even have time to play a practice round before his tee-off. Relying on the advice of locals and some tour veterans, John Daly began his four-day march to destiny.

The course was soft on the first day of the tournament. Storms had passed over the area in the morning and a lightning bolt killed a man who was getting ready to leave the course. Play resumed in the afternoon, however, and the soft fairways and softer greens played right into John Daly's game plan.

With such a big booming driver, Daly could swat the ball at will and not have to worry as much about an errant drive bouncing off the fairway into trouble. The fairways were so soft that they caught his drives and nestled them safely within their confines. Other players, however, did not like the soggy fairways. When conditions were like this, with no bounce on the fair-

Daly was still clinging to the lead on the final day of the PGA Championship. Spectators eagerly congratulated the little known golfer as he approached the 10th tee.

way, they lost a lot of distance on their drives. On that first day, John used his tremendous length off the tee to his advantage, as he was easily three to four clubs lower on his approach shots than most of his counterparts. For instance, on a par four of 445 yards, John could hit his drive and be close enough to use a wedge or nine-iron to the green. Other players, some outdriven by as much as 40 yards on average by Daly, were forced to use anywhere from a four to six iron on this kind of hole. With a high loft club on his approach shot, Daly had much more control in getting his balls on the greens, close

John Daly

Daly can hardly believe he's won after holing out on the 18th green.

to the cup. While every hole was not played out in exactly this manner, it was a recurring scenario over the whole weekend.

John finished the first day with a three-under-par 69, and was the only rookie on the leader board. He was only two shots off the lead, behind old pros Kenny Knox, Craig Stadler, and Bruce Leitzke. Literally ducking under the ropes to get into the tournament—John was the last of the alternates to be given a spot—John found himself in contention on the first day of the PGA

Championship.

While he played very well on that first day, Daly received only a bit of attention after his round. Watchers of the PGA Tour often saw rookies and unknowns do extremely well on the first day of a major and then fall back into the crowd in subsequent rounds. In the second round, however, John did even better than in the first.

As the second day wore along, and as John continued to play well, he began to attract a larger and larger gallery. Word had spread like wildfire on the course that the youngster was having another monster day, and people wanted to see him in person. Continuing to slam the golf ball, seemingly without regard for his body, his equipment, or the golf course, John regularly hit drives in excess of 300 yards; his average for the year was 286 yards per drive, but his average over the four days at Crooked Stick was 303 yards.

This was the aspect of John's game that would draw the most attention. As the fans on the South African and Ben Hogan tours knew, this was a man who could launch a golf ball. One of the most trite expressions in golf is "drive for show, putt for dough," which means that long drives really don't mean much—it is a good short game and making putts that win tournaments and prize money. Yet there is something very attractive about watching a man whack a little white ball farther than the length of three football fields. John captured the attention of the gallery at Crooked Stick with his enormous power off the tee; two days later, he would capture the attention of the entire country. He finished the day with a 67, which gave him a two-shot lead.

All eyes of the golf world were on the 25-year-old rookie from Arkansas as he started the third round, and he did not let anyone down. Although he attempted to play it safe off the first tee—he played a one-iron and took a bogey—he would not take the safe route again. Hole after hole he played his driver and continued to hit the ball as far as anyone who had ever played in a major championship. No one had ever seen a player on the tour hit the ball as far as Daly did in that weekend. No greater authority than Jack Nicklaus himself commented on television, "Good gracious! What an unleashing of power. I don't know who he reminds me of. I haven't seen anybody who hit the ball that far."

When John came off the course, he had a three-shot lead, but it was in jeopardy not from other players but from PGA officials. Someone reported that Daly's caddie had rested the flag stick on a point within a few feet of the hole when John was setting up for a long putt for eagle. The rules of golf forbid indicating the line of a putt with any object and call for a two-shot penalty. Nevertheless, the PGA ruled that there was no violation, and Daly's three-stroke lead stood.

"I just pray to God that I can go one more day," John told reporters at the end of the round. "If I can have one more day like this, I think I can bring this thing home."

Having another day "like this" was going to be a tall order for John. Being in contention for his first tour victory, in a major no less, must have really worked on John's mind. And he now faced the added pressure of playing to the largest galleries he had ever seen. Indeed, as Bruce Leitzke said, "He was getting Arnold Palmer and Jack Nicklaus-type receptions on some of the shots he was hitting out there. He was a big, big gallery favorite."

Listening to the urging of his caddie, who said "Kill" every time he handed Daly his driver, the rookie went out and made the Crooked Stick Golf Club his own that Sunday. Shooting one under for the day, a day in which he never really gave anyone an easy opportunity to catch him, John was the story on the course that afternoon in August. Bruce Leitzke was the only one who could have caught him, but he missed a number of birdie putts that would have made a ball game of it.

Even though he was in control and comfortable the whole day, after the tournament he admitted that when he reached the 16th hole, "That's when I couldn't keep telling myself it wasn't a major. I knew it was a major." As he walked up the 18th fairway to the thunderous applause of the gallery that had embraced John as a folk hero, he pumped his fist in the air, which drove the crowd to cheer even louder. His two-putt on 18 gave him a par for the hole and a 71 for the day, putting him three strokes ahead of Leitzke, five strokes in front of Jim Gallagher, and six over Kenny Knox.

When he holed out on 18, and Bettye embraced him in front of the national media, he knew that he had finally made it. At the age of 25 he had won his first major tournament, one of only a handful of players whose first tour victory was a major. Yet, as he stood on that green on a golf course in Indianapolis, he could not have known how much this victory would change his life forever. But there would be plenty of time to think about that. Right then, all he wanted to do was soak it all in and bask in the most glorious moment of his life.

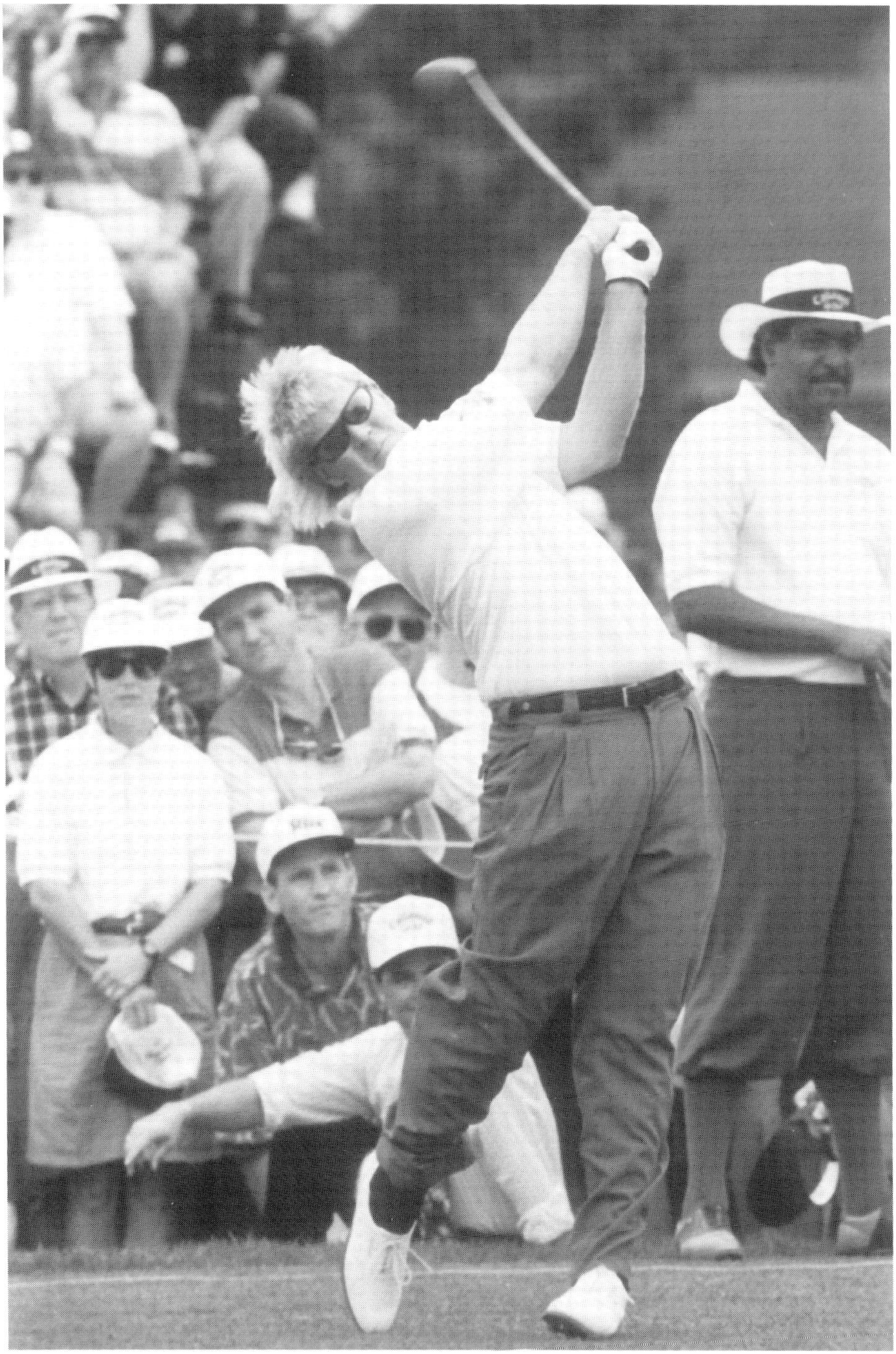

6
HAZARDS

When a rookie wins on the PGA Tour, it is usually received by the sports world with a little more fanfare than when a veteran wins; when a rookie wins a major it is much bigger news; and when a rookie wins a major in the way John Daly did, it explodes off the sports page and into the living rooms of the entire country. The last American player to make such a splash was another big hitter, a chunky kid from Ohio whose first tour victory was the U.S. Open in 1960; his name was Jack Nicklaus. To underscore how big Daly's win at Crooked Stick was, it received front-page coverage in the *New York Times*, a paper not especially known for its sports reporting. Simply put, the PGA victory made Daly a household name.

Daly unleashes another monster drive at the 1993 Shell Houston Open's Long Drive Contest. Daly won $40,000 for the long drive of 340 yards, 1 1/2 feet, and another $40,000 for the long average of 337 yards. Jim Dent, the Senior Tour's long-drive champion, is at right.

In the days and weeks that followed, Daly was in the middle of a whirlwind of activity. There were press conferences and appearances on *Larry King Live*, *The Tonight Show*, and *Good Morning America*. He appeared on the cover of *Sports Illustrated* and was featured in *People* and *Time* magazines. Indianapolis Colts coach Ron Meyer even offered to let John kick extra points in an exhibition game when he heard that John had been a kicker in high school. (Cooler heads prevailed in this situation, as Colts officials and PGA people nixed that idea.) Then Governor Bill Clinton proclaimed the Monday following the PGA to be John Daly Day in the State of Arkansas.

One reason for Daly's popularity was that he reminded the average golfer of someone he knew quite well—himself. He was a bit overweight, smoked cigarettes, and whacked the ball as hard as he could every time he stepped up to the ball. While golfers say they respect a player who can putt and control his short game, they will pay money to see a guy who can hit the ball 320 yards down the fairway. John was appealing to the golfing public for other reasons as well. Contrary to the popular conception, golf is not that much of a "rich man's game." The average player does not belong to an exclusive country club, get private lessons from a club pro, or own a $1,000 set of clubs. The average golfer most likely wakes up early in the morning to get a tee time at the local public course, carries his own bag, and is happy to make a few pars.

Moreover, with John's background and attitude on and off the course, he really spoke to these golfers more than any player since the colorful Lee Trevino did in the 1960s. John was an instant folk hero; he was someone who broke the rules and succeeded in a way no one thought possible. In the rather stuffy world of professional golf, where good manners, safe play, and a squeaky clean image were the norm, John was a breath of fresh air.

Winning the tournament meant a 10-year exemption on the PGA Tour, which meant that no matter where he finished on the money list, he would not have to go back through the torture of the qualifying tournament. It also meant winning the largest sum of money he had earned to date, a whopping $230,000, a far cry from the loose change he used to pick up on the Hogan Tour. And it brought him a lot more money in endorsement deals from major golf equipment manufacturers, such as Wilson and Reebok. The one victory virtually guaranteed that he would never be poor again.

The rest of the 1991 season was more or less uneventful for John. He did not really come close to winning another tournament, but he did become the biggest draw on the tour. No matter where he was on the leader board, he commanded huge galleries; everyone wanted to see this kid hit a golf ball, and he loved their oohs and ahs when he blasted one of his patented 320-yard moon shots.

Daly's arrival as a big-time player was confirmed by his invitation to the 1991 Skins Game, a popular television event that took place over Thanksgiving Weekend. John won the first nine holes, beating Jack Nicklaus, Payne Stewart, and Curtis Strange to pocket $120,000. In January 1992, John was awarded the 1991 Rookie of the Year award by the PGA of America.

The following year, with a number of top-10

finishes and a good showing at the Masters—he made the cut and tied for 19th at Augusta National—John continued to be the most popular player on the tour. In late September, he won the B.C. Open in Endicott, New York. This was not one of the most celebrated stops on the PGA Tour, but it was a tour victory and it kept John in the spotlight.

Wherever John went, there was a hive of activity, a lot of media, and mobs of adoring fans, but sometimes there was trouble. Off the course, John's relationship with Bettye had been up and down. All sorts of rumors sprang up about the two of them. Some reports said that they were having problems, some said that Bettye was actually older than she said, had not yet divorced her estranged husband, and had a 14-year-old son. There were other reports that John was again having trouble controlling his drinking. Whatever the rumors, John and Bettye were still together, were in love with each other, and even bought a house together in Castle Pines, Colorado.

The house became the focal point of the first of John Daly's off-the-course troubles. One night during a Christmas party, he and Bettye had a number of friends over. John had been drinking heavily, and by the end of the night, the local sheriffs arrived at a wrecked house and were greeted by a shaken-up Bettye. In a drunken rage, John had lost control and made a mess of his own house. Although he had been drunk and had been involved in incidents before, he had never had to answer to the police. This time he did. Pleading to a misdemeanor harassment charge, he accepted two years' probation with the requirement that he undergo alcohol reha-

Daly is besieged by autograph seekers during a practice round at the U.S. Open.

bilitation. After all the years of partying and abusing alcohol, John had hit bottom. He was also suspended from the tour.

Soon after the court ruling, John spent three weeks at a rehab facility in Arizona. At Sierra Tucson, John met an alcohol counselor who had played professional football in the 1970s. Thomas "Hollywood" Henderson was a linebacker for the Dallas Cowboys during their glory days; he had two Super Bowl rings to show for his time in the NFL, but not much else. He had lost just about everything he had to a monster cocaine addiction. After finally cleaning himself up, he became a counselor in order to help other people with the same problems he had. Who could have been a better adviser to Daly than Henderson? They both knew a lot about using substances to help take the edge off the pressure of

Daly waits for the action to resume at a Mexican tournament in 1993. Daly was under suspension from the PGA at the time.

being a professional athlete. The two would remain in contact long after Daly left Tucson.

Although Daly had a good friend in Henderson to help him through the rough spots, he was taking on his problem pretty much on his own. Substituting his own program for any conventional program, such as Alcoholics Anonymous, John rejoined the tour in January 1993 and played well in some of the early tournaments. Crediting his good standing to switching from beer and whiskey to peanut M&Ms, John played the rest of the spring and summer of 1993 without a tour victory, but with good showings at a number of them, including third place at the Masters in April.

A sober John Daly was going to absolutely rule

the PGA Tour, or so thought many of the people who followed golf at the time. However, that just did not happen. As a matter of fact, a number of incidents that season pointed to just the opposite; John did not seem to be handling things as well on the course.

There were a number of episodes in 1993 that led to a second suspension. In August, he got bored waiting to hit his second shot at a tournament in Portland and shot a ball over the heads of an onlooking gallery. Next, he refused to sign his scorecard at another tournament, thereby disqualifying himself. In September, he just out-and-out quit at the Southern Open; a few weeks later he did the same thing at the Kapula International in Hawaii. The PGA prided itself on its clean-cut image, and John Daly was making a lot of people angry: his fellow golfers, the sponsors, and especially PGA officials. In November, they had had enough and suspended Daly indefinitely.

About this same time, John filed for divorce. After three years, in which he and Bettye spent as much time fighting as they did happy together, John knew that his marriage was over. After the Colorado incident, it was only a matter of time. Among John's biggest regrets about the divorce was most likely the fact that he would no longer get to see his daughter Shynah on a regular basis. But, as he told *Sports Illustrated*, "We finally agreed we just wanted to do what's best for her."

With a divorce hanging on him, a suspension ahead of him, and without alcohol to help him through, it would not have surprised anyone if John had sunk into a long depression during his suspension. However, he did just the opposite. Knowing his future was riding on the next few months, he went back to his home, just outside of Orlando, Florida, and practiced golf, played the guitar, and worked out. Overweight from his alcohol-free M&M-filled diet, John was once again approaching his freshman year bulk at Arkansas. During his suspension, however, he took control of his life, ate right, and got himself into much better shape, both mentally and physically. Four months after his suspension, he was reinstated by PGA commissioner Deane Beman.

The divorce and two suspensions caused John to lose his "folk hero" status. Even though he was still a huge attraction on the course, he was no longer a breath of fresh air on the tour. One writer for *USA Today* said he was "an ill wind."

For someone with such a gift for golf, John seemed to lack the ability to make good decisions at critical times. However, as a rule, John was one of the most charming and giving people on the tour. For instance, John was known as one of the few players who would actually stop and give autographs, many times signing until everyone had been taken care of. Then there is the story of an eight-year-old girl selling golf balls on a course in Memphis in order to save money for college. She approached John, and, not knowing who he was, asked him if he would like to buy some. He reached into his pocket and gave her some folded bills. When she gave him the balls, he told her to keep them, he had enough. Then he signed a new one of his own and gave it to the girl. When the girl finally unfolded the bills, she realized that John Daly had given her $300. Finally, there was the $30,000 he donated to the fund for the family of a man who was struck by lightning at the PGA Championship in 1991.

Perhaps the only thing that rivaled his big heart was his capacity to hurt himself. However, after his suspension, he looked to the future, and seemed to have a renewed sense of himself and his approach to his game. He told *Sports Illustrated*, "I've got a lot of stuff off my back. It's like starting all over again." It was indeed a new John Daly who pronounced, "My dream when I was a kid was coming out here and winning. I want to get back to that dream."

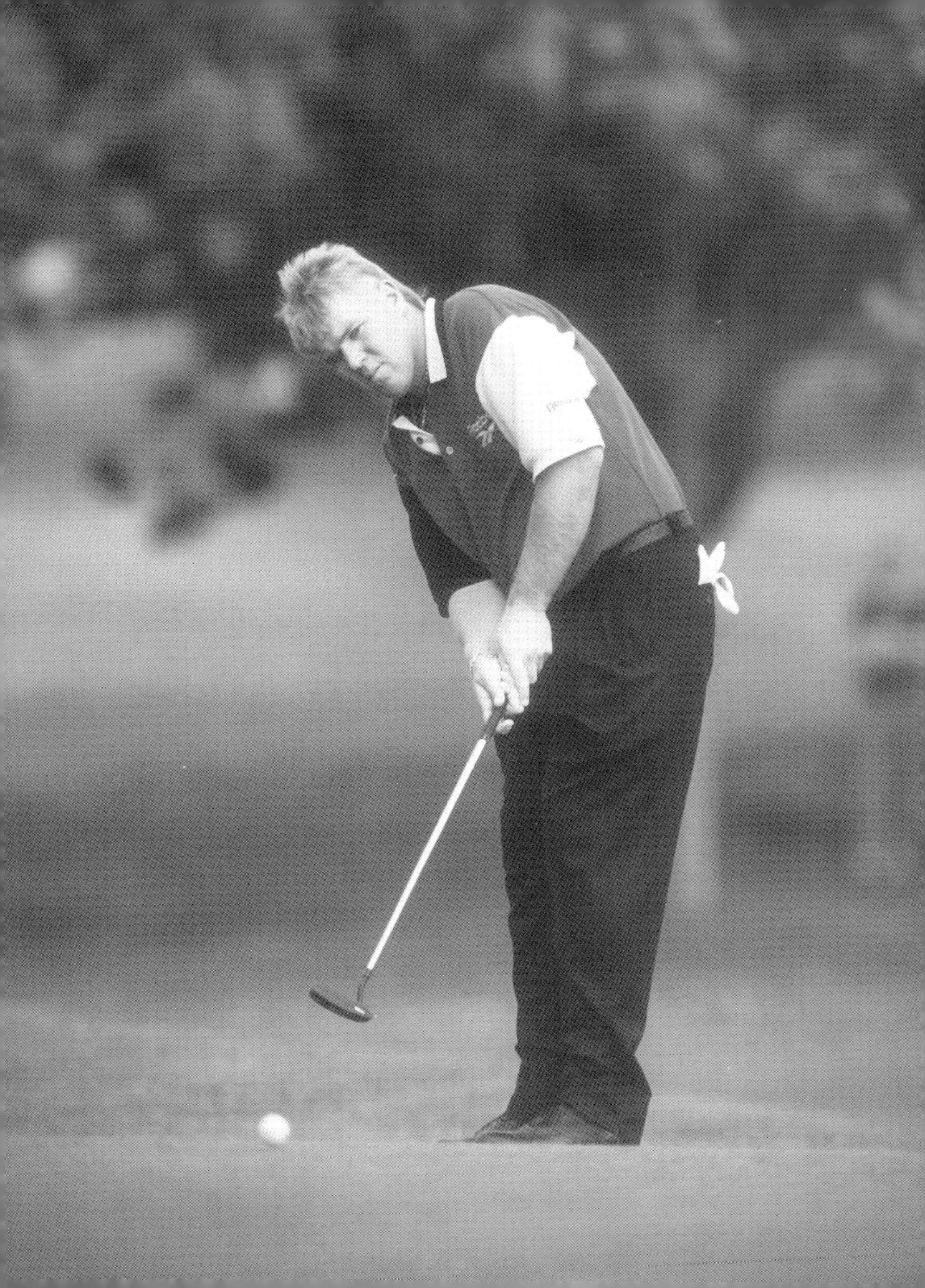

7

THE LONG ROAD BACK

Returning to the tour after a four-month suspension in March 1994, John was going to be scrutinized more than he had ever been before: by the media, by the PGA, and by his fans. He knew that any wrong move, any late night out, any breach of etiquette on the golf course was going to be blown out of proportion and would likely land him back in the PGA offices again.

His first tournament was the Honda Classic in Fort Lauderdale, and after a four-month lay-off, he took fourth place. John Daly was back.

Daly removed all doubt about his presence on the tour with his gutsy and mature performance at the BellSouth Classic in Atlanta. This was a true test of John's golf willpower. The course at the Atlanta Country Club contained very narrow fairways, and it was all John could do to keep the driver in his bag. Hitting irons off the

---

Daly knew that the crowds and media would be watching him carefully when he returned from his suspensions. Here he sinks a 40-foot putt for birdie at the 1995 Nissan Open.

tee was the smart play at this course, but for the big-swinging John Daly, playing his irons had never been part of his game. In addition to that conflict, John also had to listen to the fans, who were quite disappointed that he hit his driver only occasionally. Nevertheless, John stuck to his plan, stayed out of trouble, and by the end of the third round, he led the tournament by two strokes. On Sunday, John extended the lead to four strokes, but he squandered it down the stretch. By the 18th hole he found himself in a tie for the lead.

Approaching the 18th tee, John made his decision about how he was going to play the hole. Seeing that the safe play was not working this day, he took out his old friend the "big dog," his trusty driver. The roar of the gallery was deafening. This was the John Daly they had lined up to see, and when he swatted a 320-yard missile down the fairway, they went absolutely crazy. After he putted out for a birdie on the hole, the tournament was his. It was a different John Daly who addressed reporters that Sunday afternoon. "It's a great win," he told them, "knowing how hard I worked before I came out. I can honestly say it's the first time I've won a PGA tournament in a sober manner. It's a great feeling knowing I can win sober."

Following his victory at the BellSouth Tournament, John was again highly in demand. He was so sought after that he reworked his endorsement deal with the folks at Wilson into a 10-year, $30-million contract. It was one of the most lavish endorsements in the history of the game.

The rest of that summer, John played with varying amounts of success. He played fairly well at the Masters, finishing in the top 50, but he missed the cut at the U.S. Open.

John played well during the early rounds at the 1994 British Open, leading the tournament at one point on Friday. However, even though he made the cut, he played horrendously on Saturday and Sunday, and finished dead last.

When he returned to the States, he began to experience back problems, which came as no surprise to anyone who had ever seen him coil his body up before he hit the ball. Sidelined by his back injury that fall, John went back to the University of Arkansas to help Bill Woodley as an assistant coach on the golf team. Woodley was glad to have an opportunity to have one of the game's premiere professionals on his staff, and John was happy to help out.

Once his back started to feel better, John played a number of tournaments in the West and in Australia before hitting the tour full tilt in the spring of 1995.

His first major of the year was the Masters in Augusta, Georgia. The classic, "old boy" tournament, the Masters would give John huge galleries, but not the kind of howling rowdy behavior he thrived on. He was able to make the cut, but he only finished tied for 45th place. The rest of the spring was much the same way for John.

For the first time in his professional career, things in John's personal life were going great. He was not drinking anymore, he had married Paulette Dean the previous spring, and they were preparing for the birth of their daughter, Sierra.

The question might have been justly asked of John: why even go to the British Open? In three previous appearances there he had played horribly. However, John had a good feeling about the Old Course at St. Andrews, telling reporters

Daly remains one of the most talented golfers on the tour. Here he tips his hat to the cheering crowd after winning the 1994 BellSouth Classic.

"This is a course I love more than any other, because it is so much fun." John's love of the course combined with the total lack of pressure on him to win—he was a 66-1 underdog according to London bookmakers—produced one of the British Open's most memorable championships.

The 1995 British Open stands as a testament to the sheer will and unadulterated power of John Daly's game. This was the type of game that made him a household name far beyond the golfing world. The distance he hit balls became the stuff of legend on the PGA tour; indeed, every golfer has his favorite John Daly story. (Such as the one where officials at the Masters raised the netting at the practice range some 20 feet to prevent John from hitting any balls onto the adjoining road; John hit five or six over it anyway.)

The Long Road Back

John's turnaround as a member of the tour did not go unnoticed by his fellow golfers. Before the Sunday playoff at the British Open, tour veterans Corey Pavin, Bob Estes, and Brad Faxon all came around to give John a pat on the back. In addition, Mark Brooks, another tour member, lent his yardage book to Daly, who had lost his own in all the confusion before the playoff. It must have been a gratifying feeling for Daly, whose career had seemed like one long bungee cord ride, constantly bouncing up and down. It was a new John Daly who told reporters, "I think if I just keep on doing what I'm doing, on the course and off it, then everything is going to be okay."

The 1996 season was one that John would probably have liked to forget; he finished 121st on the money list and missed nine cuts. Trying to find the right balance between control and great power, John experimented with something Wilson Sporting Goods invented, called the Zero Iron, which John hit off the tee instead of a driver in 1996. Getting used to the club proved to be a season-long process for John, and he paid the price. His woes continued in 1997, as he was again suspended for drinking problems, and his marriage fell apart. Reebok decided against renewing its contract with Daly and Wilson ended its deal with John, although Callaway Golf signed him to a large contract to promote their clubs. The low point of the year came when a shaky Daly walked off the course at the U.S. Open without even telling his partners that he was quitting. Still, only a few months later, a sizzling first round at the British Open gave him the lead and showed he had lost none of his enormous talent.

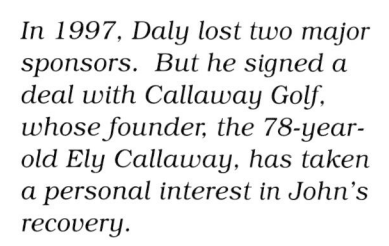

In 1997, Daly lost two major sponsors. But he signed a deal with Callaway Golf, whose founder, the 78-year-old Ely Callaway, has taken a personal interest in John's recovery.

For anyone who has ever seen him play; anyone who has witnessed one of his gargantuan drives followed by a skillful approach shot and birdie putt; anyone who has ever gone to the driving range to hit a ball as hard as he can, just to play like him, John Daly will always be a celebrated figure on the PGA tour. He is one of the most colorful figures to walk the sod in 30 years, and John Daly—win, lose, or draw—will remain among the most popular golfers of his time, perhaps of all time.

STATISTICS

Golf keeps as many statistics as any other sport. Below are just some of the figures John Daly amassed during 1997. They prove Daly is not merely terrific with the driver, he's also a fine putter and outstanding with the sand wedge.

Category	Explanation	Statistic	PGA Rank
Driving Length	Average length of drives off the tee (in yards)	309.8	1st
Driving Accuracy	Hit 122 fairways out of a possible 238	51.3%	142nd
Greens in Regulation	Hit 205 of possible 306 greens without falling a stroke behind	67.0%	65th
Putting Accuracy	Took 355 putts on 205 greens reached in regulation	1.732	10th
Eagles	Number of eagles (two under par on a hole)	4	14th
Eagle Percentage	Had 4 eagles in 306 holes	1.3%	5th
Birdies	Number of birdies (one under par on a hole)	77	71st
Birdie Percentage	Had 77 birdies in 17 rounds	4.53	6th
Birdie Conversion	Made 77 birdies on 205 greens reached in regulation	37.6	3rd
Sand Saves	Saved 25 balls hit in 32 bunkers	78.1%	1st
Par Breakers	Had 81 birdies and eagles in 306 holes	26.5%	4th
Putts Per Round	Took 484 putts in 17 rounds	28.47	19th
Scoring Average	Took 1200 strikes in 17 rounds	70.59	35th
Scoring Average Before Cut	Took 844 strikes in 12 rounds	70.33	39th
Money Earned	Total prize money earned	$61,875	70th

At the end of the season, Daly had won $2,085,043 in prize money over the course of his career. That ranked him 104th of all current PGA players.

CHRONOLOGY

1966   Is born on March 23.

1983   Leads his high school team to the state championship; wins the Missouri Amateur Championship.

1984   Wins the Arkansas Amateur Championship; enrolls at the University of Alabama.

1987   Leaves University of Alabama to turn pro.

1990   Wins his first tournament—in Sunshine Tour in Swaziland.

1991   Wins his first American tournament and his first major—the PGA—after initially being placed ninth on the invitee waiting list; wins $120,000 in the Skins Game and is named Rookie of the Year.

1992   Wins the B.C. Open, but is suspended at the end of the year for alcohol problems.

1993   Is suspended by the PGA for four months.

1994   Wins the BellSouth Tournament.

1995   Wins second major, the British Open, in a playoff against Constantino Rocca.

1997   Alcohol problems lead to another PGA suspension and the loss of most of Daly's corporate sponsors; however, Daly shows he is still a formidable golfer and crowd pleaser.

FURTHER READING

Daly, John, with John Andrisani. *Grip It and Rip It: John Daly's Guide to Hitting the Ball Farther Than You Ever Have Before.* New York: HarperCollins Publishers, 1992.

Feinstein, John. "The Daly Experience." *Golf Magazine*, August, 1994.

Johnson, Ray, S. "A Troubled Athlete's Last Chance." *Fortune*, July 7, 1997.

Reilly, Rick. "An Epic Finish." *Sports Illustrated*, August 31, 1995.

Reilly, Rick. "Playing a New Tune." *Sports Illustrated*, March 14, 1994.

Wartman, William. *John Daly: Wild Thing.* New York: HarperCollins Publishers, 1996.

ABOUT THE AUTHOR

Martin Mooney earned his A.B. at Dartmouth College and is the assistant director of college advising at The Hill School in Pottstown, Pennsylvania, where he lives with his wife, Danielle, two daughters, Katherine and Megan, and various pets. A former editor of children's books, he is also the author of *The Comanche Indians* in Chelsea House's Junior Library of American Indians and *Brett Favre* in the Football Legends series.

INDEX

Anderson, Tip, 36-37, 39
Beman, Deane, 52
Brooks, Mark, 59
Callaway, Ely, 60
Campbell, Michael, 9
Cassmeyer, Scott, 17
Clinton, Bill, 46
Crofton, Dale, 33
Daly, Jamie, 21, 22
Daly, Jim, 15, 16, 22
Daly, John
   as a football player, 15, 18-19
   honors received, 29, 47
   nickname of, 15
   troubles with alcohol, 19, 27, 33, 48-49
Daly, Paulette, 7, 12, 57
Daly, Shynah, 51
Daly, Sierra, 57
Dent, Jim, 45
Estes, Bob, 59
Faxon, Brad, 8, 59
Fulford, Bettye, 32, 35, 37, 38, 43, 48, 51
Gallagher, Jim, 43
Glasson, Bill, 10

Hengtes, Chris, 17, 18, 19, 21
Hengtes, Ray, 16, 17, 18
Henderson, Thomas "Hollywood," 49-50
King, Larry, 46
Knox, Kenny, 40, 43
Leitzke, Bruce, 40, 42, 43
Love, Davis, III, 11
Loy, Steve, 21, 23, 24, 26
Meyer, Ron, 46
Nicklaus, Jack, 10, 25, 33, 42, 45, 47
Pavin, Corey, 59
Pickett, Wilson, 7
Price, Nick, 38
Rocca, Constantino, 9, 10, 11-12, 13
Ross, Rick, 22
Stadler, Craig, 40
Stewart, Payne, 47
Strange, Curtis, 47
Struttman, Brad, 17
Tomori, Katsuyoshi, 8
Trevino, Lee, 47
Woodley, Bill, 25, 26-27, 29, 57
Zoeller, Fuzzy, 35

PHOTO CREDITS:
AP/Wide World Photos: pp. 2, 6, 10, 13, 32, 36, 39, 40, 44, 49, 50, 54, 58 ; courtesy Brother James Abell: pp. 14, 18; courtesy Ray Hentges: p. 17; courtesy University of Arkansas: pp. 20, 25; Greg Bell/University of Arkansas: p. 26; Arkansas Democrat-Gazette: 28; courtesy Callaway Golf: 60.